BUILD YOUR OWN LAND VEHICLES

Thanks to the creative team:
Senior Editor: Alice Peebles
Fact checking: Tom Jackson
Design: Perfect Bound Ltd

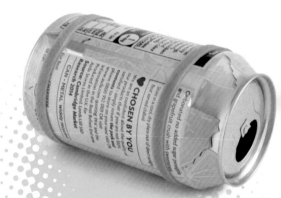

Hungry Tomato®
A division of Lerner Publishing Group, Inc.
241 First Avenue North
Minneapolis, MN 55401 USA

For reading levels and more information, look up this title at www.lernerbooks.com.

Main body text set in Neutraliser Serif Regular 9.75/13.

Library of Congress Cataloging-in-Publication Data

The Cataloging-in-Publication Data for *Build Your Own Land Vehicles* is on file at the Library of Congress.
ISBN 978-1-5124-5968-5 (lib. bdg.)
ISBN 978-1-5124-9870-7 (EB pdf)

Manufactured in the United States of America
1-43027-27696-9/13/2017

BUILD YOUR OWN LAND VEHICLES

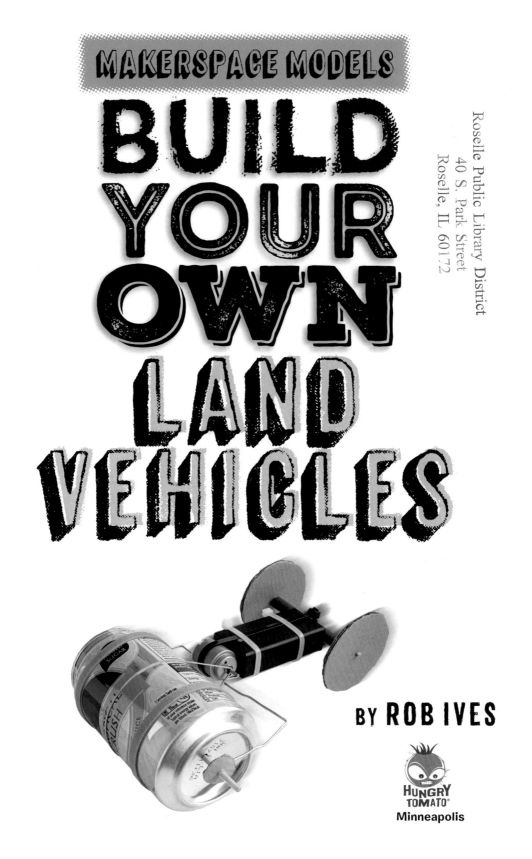

BY **ROB IVES**

HUNGRY TOMATO®
Minneapolis

SAFETY FIRST

Take care and use good sense when making these fun model vehicles. They are all straightforward, but some activities call for cutting materials, drilling holes, and other skills for which you should ask an adult assistant for help (see below).

Every project includes a list of supplies that you will need. Most will be stuff that you can find around the house or that can be bought inexpensively online or at a local hardware store.

We have also included "How It Works" for each model, which explains, in simple terms, the engineering or scientific principles that make the model move. For some, there is a "Real-World Engineering" snippet that applies these principles to actual machines.

Watch out for this sign accompanying some model instructions. You may need help from an adult with completing these tasks.

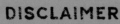

CONTENTS

LAND VEHICLES

When you're out riding in the car with your mom and dad, the car seems to change speed really easily, doesn't it? Your mom or dad just uses the accelerator or brake pedals to speed up or slow down. But there's so much work going on under the hood, and it's all at the command of the driver pushing the pedals and moving the gearshift.

Now you can get into the driver's seat with these eight amazing models. These models operate on the idea that nothing moves unless it's pushed by a force! And you don't need a car engine to do that. A twisted rubber band will do the job. Combine it with two clothespins, and you have a tiny dragster. Or add a mini motor to give extra oomph to your electric car. Even the force released by an inflated balloon produces something very like rocket power.

So get your tools and materials together, start building, and see how these machines go. You can even make a mousetrap move! Let's kick off with the bouncy ball car—it shows you how car **gears** work . . .

TOP TIPS

- Before you start on any of the models, read the step-by-step instructions all the way through so you have an idea of what you're aiming for. The pictures show what the steps tell you to do.

- Use a cutting mat or similar surface for cutting lengths off skewers, etc.

- Ask for help with cutting the barrel of a pen—this can be very tricky! One way of cutting it neatly is to use a file to score a notch all the way around, then snap off the piece.

- Use the sharp end of a pencil to make small holes in cardboard. Or, better yet, ask an adult to help, using scissors or a utility knife.

TOOL KIT

- Ruler (long and standard)
- Utlilty knife
- File
- Gaffer tape (or duct tape)
- Clear tape
- Needle-nose pliers
- Craft drill
- Compass
- Wire cutters
- White glue
- Super glue
- Scissors
- Cutting mat

WHITE GLUE

SUPER GLUE

BOUNCY BALL CAR

A motorized ball gives a whole new meaning to ball control! It's pushed along by a small companion wheel.

TOOLS:
- Scissors
- Ruler
- Super glue
- File
- Wire cutters
- Needle-nose pliers

YOU WILL NEED:

Battery-powered handheld electric fan

Four zip ties

Two wooden chopsticks

Wide rubber bands

Ballpoint pen

Two roundhead screws 0.5 in. x 0.2 in. (13 x 5 mm)

Smooth 9-in. (220 mm) plastic ball

Two rubber suction cups, 1.7 in. wide (40 mm) such as from a shower soap dish

Two plastic airflow golf balls

Stiff 0.08-in. (2 mm) garden wire

PULL

1 Pull the fan head off the electric fan, revealing the electric motor shaft.

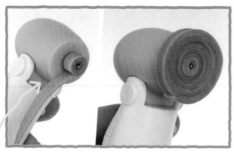

2 Cut a rubber band and carefully wrap it around the motor shaft, gluing it in place with super glue at the same time. Continue adding rubber bands until the rubber wheel is roughly 2 in. (50 mm) in diameter.

3 Twist a screw into the end of the suction cups so the head of the screw is about 0.2 in. (5 mm) above the top of the suction cup. Add a dot of glue to the screw as you twist it in to keep the seal airtight.

4 Wet the suction cups and stick them to either side of the ball. Get them as exactly opposite from each other as possible.

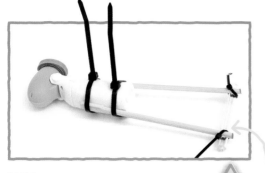

6 Use wire cutters to cut a length of wire three times the diameter of the ball. Use pliers to make a loop at one end to fit over the screw. Shape the rest of the wire as in the image below, so it slides through one golf ball, the pen tube, and the other golf ball. Make another loop at the other end to fit the opposite screw.

The wheel and ball should rotate in the directions shown below. If not, flip the motor over to the other side of the ball.

5 Discard the ink cartridge from the ballpoint pen. Cut a 2-in. (50 mm) section from the pen body with a file (see Top Tips, page 6). Fasten the chopsticks tightly to the fan body with zip ties. Tie the pen tube to the other ends using the remaining zip ties. Trim the zip tie ends with scissors.

Start up the fan motor. Place the vehicle on a smooth, flat surface (not a carpet), rest the rubber wheel on the ball and watch it being driven!

ZOOOOM!

HOW IT WORKS

The ball model is powered by an electric motor. **Chemical energy** from the battery is converted into **electrical energy** and then into spinning **kinetic energy** by the electric motor. The small rubber-band wheel and the large ball work together like a gear slowing down the final rotation, so the vehicle moves in a controlled way. The rubber-band wheel is held against the ball by **gravity**.

The gears on a car are also round and different sizes, but have toothed edges to grip one another.

ROCKET POWER

This car shoots off as the balloon loses air. It uses the same principle as rocket power: a thrust backward creates a push forward.

TOOLS:
- Ruler
- Utility knife
- Craft drill
- File
- Gaffer tape (or duct tape)
- Scissors

YOU WILL NEED:

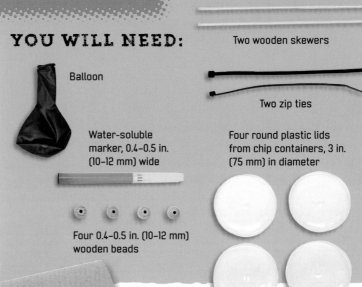

Balloon

Water-soluble marker, 0.4–0.5 in. (10–12 mm) wide

Four 0.4–0.5 in. (10–12 mm) wooden beads

Thin poster tube, 2 in. (50 mm) wide

Two wooden skewers

Two zip ties

Four round plastic lids from chip containers, 3 in. (75 mm) in diameter

1 Use a craft knife to cut an 8-in (200 mm) length of poster tube. Use a craft drill to drill holes slightly larger than the skewers on opposite sides, roughly 1.5 in. (40 mm) from each end.

2 Cut two 3.5 in. (90 mm) lengths of skewer for the **axles**. Make a small hole with a utility knife in the center of the lids to fit the skewers tightly. Thread the skewers into the tube. Add a bead on each side as a washer.

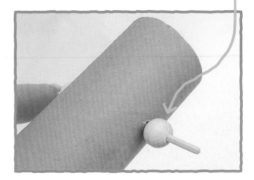

3 Fit the lid wheels onto the skewers, with the rims facing outward.

4 Remove the pen top and cut a 2.8-in (70 mm) section from the body with a file. The inner cartridge will drop out.

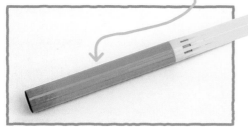

5 Fit the end of the balloon over the wider end of the pen. Tape it in place with gaffer tape.

6 Position the pen section on the poster tube so that it extends beyond the end of the tube by 0.4 in. (10 mm). Secure it in place with two zip ties. Trim the ends of the ties with scissors.

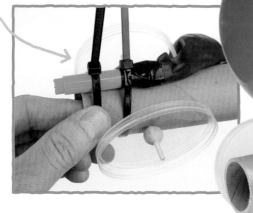

7 Inflate the balloon by blowing into the pen nozzle. Pinch the balloon end above the nozzle, place the rocket car on a smooth surface, and . . .

. . . release!

WHOOSH!

HOW IT WORKS

When the balloon is released, the elastic of the balloon pushes air out of the nozzle, and the car shoots forward, just like a rocket! It's an example of **Newton's Third Law of Motion**: every action has an equal and opposite reaction. So a rocket shoots out burning gases (the action) with a force to give it liftoff (the reaction).

ELECTRIC CAN CAR

The Model T Ford got the nickname Tin Lizzie in 1922, when it beat lots of fancier cars in a race—but people thought it looked like a tin can! This tin-can car can really go too!

TOOLS:

- Long ruler
- Compass
- Kitchen scissors
- Clear tape
- Craft drill
- File
- Wire cutters
- Needle-nose pliers
- White glue

YOU WILL NEED:

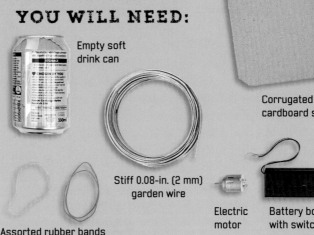

Empty soft drink can

Corrugated cardboard scraps

Stiff 0.08-in. (2 mm) garden wire

Assorted rubber bands

Electric motor

Battery box with switch

Three zip ties

Thin markers, roughly 0.3 in. (8 mm) in diameter

Two wooden skewers

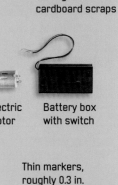

1 Rinse out and thoroughly dry the drink can. Find two wide rubber bands that fit tightly around the can. These will act as tires.

2 Measure the diameter of the open end of the can. With a compass and scissors, cut a circle of corrugated cardboard to fit just inside the rim of the can. Make a hole in the center of the cardboard with a skewer. Tape the circle in place.

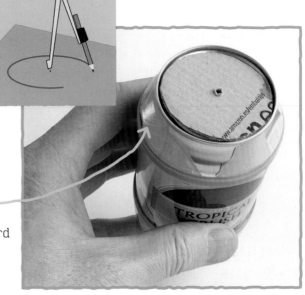

3 Make a hole in the center of the other end of the can with a craft drill. Thread a wooden skewer through the bottom of the can and up through the cardboard circle.

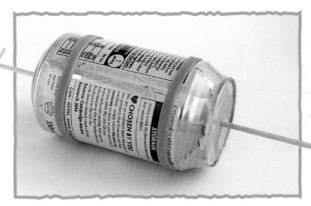

4 Connect the battery box to the motor and give it a test run. The shaft on the motor will be the drive shaft. Keep the battery and motor connected.

5 Cut a 3-in. (80 mm) length of marker tube with a file. Use a zip tie to wrap together the motor, battery, and tube. Trim the tie with scissors.

6 Fit a loose-fitting, thin rubber band around the can between the other two rubber bands. This will be your drive belt.

The mounting carriage is slightly off-center, so the drive shaft from the motor is close to the center.

7 Use wire cutters to cut a length of garden wire about 24 in. (600 mm) long. Use pliers to form a loop at each end and to shape it as shown to make a mounting carriage for the motor. Slot the loops over the skewer.

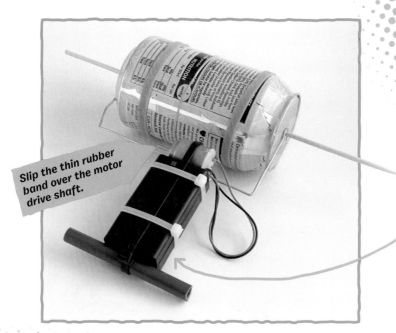

Slip the thin rubber band over the motor drive shaft.

8 Use two zip ties to secure the motor and the battery onto the mounting carriage. Trim the ends of the ties.

9 Draw and cut four cardboard circles, roughly 2 in. (50 mm) in diameter. Glue them in pairs with white glue to make the wheels. Make holes in the centers with a skewer. Slot the skewer through the pen tube and fit on the wheels.

10 Make two cardboard washers, 0.8 in. (20 mm) in diameter. Fit them over the can skewer to keep the wire in place. Trim all the skewer ends with wire cutters.

Start the motor and see how your electric can... can GO!

VVRRRMMM!

HOW IT WORKS

The battery powers the motor to spin its shaft, turning the thin rubber band to move the can. The thick rubber bands around the can work like tires. Rubber has a high coefficient of **friction**, meaning it firmly grips only the surface it is resting on. The small drive shaft of the motor, the body of the can, and the thin rubber band work as the drive system.

REAL-WORLD ENGINEERING

When a car engine is turned on, fuel burns and becomes a hot gas, which expands. The energy from the expanding gas pushes down pistons in the engine and creates kinetic energy—energy from movement. Kinetic energy is transferred through the drive system to the wheels to make them rotate.

15

DYNAMIC DRAGSTER

The power from a stretched rubber band mimics the dramatic acceleration of dragsters: cars that race over very short distances.

TOOLS:
- Ruler
- Wire cutters
- Needle-nose pliers
- Scissors

YOU WILL NEED:

Stiff 0.08 in. (2 mm) garden wire

Assorted rubber bands

Two 0.4–0.5 in. (10-12 mm) wooden beads

Two hollow 3-in. (65 mm) plastic balls

Wooden skewer

1 Pierce holes in opposite sides of the balls with the point of the skewer. Make sure the balls will fit tightly on the skewer.

POKE

2 Use wire cutters to cut a 12-in. (300 mm) length of wire. Thread wooden beads onto the wire. Shape wire with pliers into a square-ended U to hold the beads. Make small loops at the ends. Thread the skewer through the balls and the wire loops.

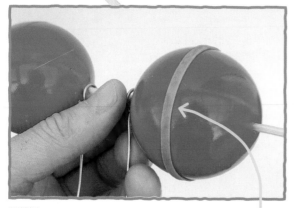

3 For the tires, choose two wide rubber bands that fit neatly around the center of the balls.

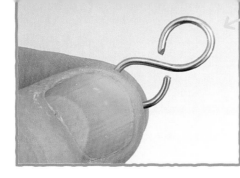

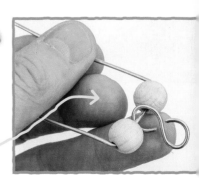

4 Cut a 2-in. (50 mm) length of wire and use the pliers to bend it into an S-shape.

5 Fit the S wire between the two beads.

6 Select a long, wide rubber band and cut it open. Tie one end securely to the free end of the S wire.

7 Wrap the other end tightly around the skewer. Roll the wheels to stretch the band so that it's under tension.

Release the band to launch your dragster!

POW!

HOW IT WORKS

Dragsters **accelerate** as fast as possible, usually for just 1,000 ft. (305 m) to reach the finish line. Energy in this model is stored in the stretched rubber band. When the dragster is released, a **restoring force** returns the band to its unstretched length. This force spins the wheels, so the model whizzes away.

MOVING MOUSETRAP

Relative to its size, the spring in a mousetrap is energy-packed. It has to be to catch mice! Here you harness that snappy speed by turning it into a car!

TOOLS:

- Craft drill
- Ruler
- Kitchen scissors
- Clear tape
- White glue
- Compass
- Needle-nose pliers

YOU WILL NEED:

Old-style wooden mousetrap

Craft sticks

Corrugated cardboard scraps

Wooden skewer

String

Assorted rubber bands

Two large paper clips

Two 0.5-in. (12 mm) flathead screws and two 0.6-in. (15 mm) washers

1 Using a craft drill, make a hole in the end of the craft sticks slightly wider than the skewer.

Cut a 2.8-in. (70 mm) length of cardboard slightly narrower than the base of the mousetrap. Cut a 2.8-in. (70 mm) length of skewer for the axle. Wrap the cardboard tightly around it and tape it in place.

Fit the axle and craft sticks together. Glue the sticks to the sides of the mousetrap with glue. Use rubber bands to hold it all in place as it dries.

Axle

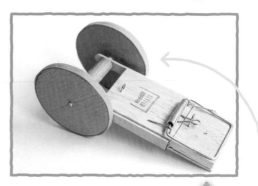

2 Cut out six 2.8-in. (70 mm) cardboard circles. Glue them in threes back-to-back to make two wheels. Choose rubber bands wide enough to wrap around the wheels as tires.

3 Using the tip of the scissors, make holes in the center of the wheels to fit snugly over the axle ends. Glue the wheels to the axle.

4 Cut out and glue two 1.6-in. (40 mm) circles of cardboard for the front wheel. Fit it with an axle made from a 1.6-in. (40 mm) length of skewer. Use pliers to straighten out the paper clips and make a loop at one end of each. Slot the loops over the axle.

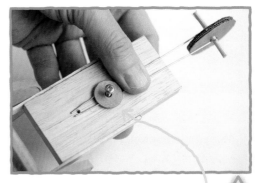

5 Drill a small pilot hole centrally in the mousetrap base and another 1.2 in. (30 mm) away. Screw in the two washers to trap the paper clip wires and to hold the front wheel in place.

7 Wrap the string around the axle, pulling it so that the swing arm pulls back. Fit the trigger in the normal way for a mousetrap. Be careful! It could bite!

6 Tie an 8-in. (200 mm) length of string to the swing arm of the mousetrap.

SNAP!

Tap the trigger with a pencil or chopstick— and launch!

Trigger

HOW IT WORKS

All vehicles work by converting some sort of stored energy into kinetic energy (energy from movement). In the mousetrap, the steel spring works as the energy store. When the mousetrap is triggered, it pulls the string wrapped around the axle, which spins the wheels and propels the car forward.

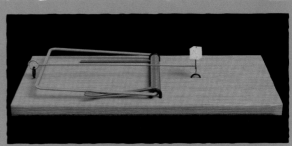

CLOTHESPIN MICRO CAR

One clothespin is the car. The other is the trigger that catapults the car into movement. Try it out on a smooth surface—make more than one and have a race!

TOOLS:
- Needle-nose pliers
- Wire cutters
- Utility knife
- White glue

YOU WILL NEED:

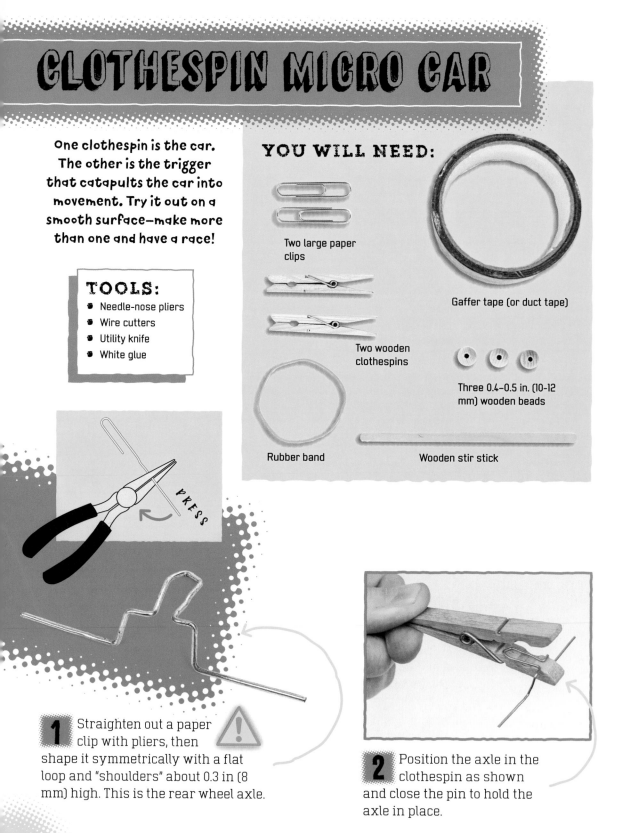

Two large paper clips

Two wooden clothespins

Rubber band

Gaffer tape (or duct tape)

Three 0.4–0.5 in. (10-12 mm) wooden beads

Wooden stir stick

PRESS

1 Straighten out a paper clip with pliers, then shape it symmetrically with a flat loop and "shoulders" about 0.3 in (8 mm) high. This is the rear wheel axle.

2 Position the axle in the clothespin as shown and close the pin to hold the axle in place.

20

3 Straighten out the second paper clip and thread it through one of the wooden beads. Using the pliers, fold the paper clip to make a flat-bottomed U-shape holding the bead. This is the front axle.

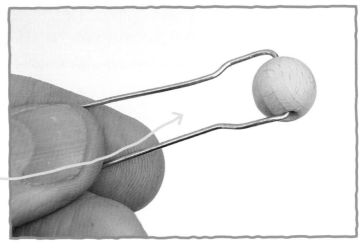

4 Use wire cutters to ⚠ trim the paper clip wire to fit along the edges of the other end of the clothespin. Tape it in place with gaffer tape. (The rear axle is not shown here.)

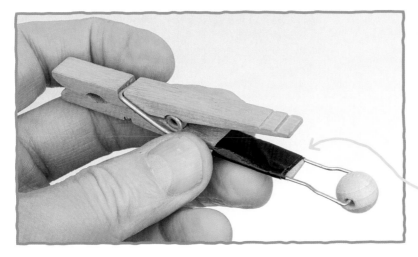

5 With the rear axle ⚠ in position, slot the wooden beads on either side of the rear axle. Bend up the ends of the wire to hold the beads in place. Snip off the excess wire with wire cutters.

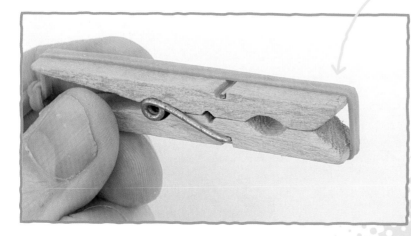

6 Cut a length of wooden stir stick slightly longer than the clothespin. Cut a notch in one end with a utility knife and glue it to the base of the clothespin as shown.

7 Wrap a rubber band around the second clothespin, tying the end if necessary to make it tight. This acts as the trigger.

8 Push the end of the wooden stir stick into the rubber band and hold it with the clothespin. Press the clothespin open to launch your car!

HOW IT WORKS

The power that drives this car is separate from the car itself. A quick elastic kick from the trigger shoots the vehicle on its way. The wire axles and bead wheels have very low friction, so after the initial kick, the car runs for a surprising distance.

KEK-POW!

REAL-WORLD ENGINEERING

An elastic material is one that can be deformed a lot but always springs back to its original shape. This is why a hand-held catapult uses an elastic band. The elastic is stretched backward to make it as tight as possible. This stretching stores energy in the band. When the band is released, it pings back into shape, and the energy is transferred to the **projectile** as kinetic energy, so it flies off.

PROPELLER POWER

If propellers give aircraft liftoff and keep them in the air, why not harness that power to move a car? In fact, an inventor named Clifford Robbins did just that in 1955. He attached a large propeller to the back of a small car to get it to speeds of 70 mph (113 km/h)—though it also had a small engine!

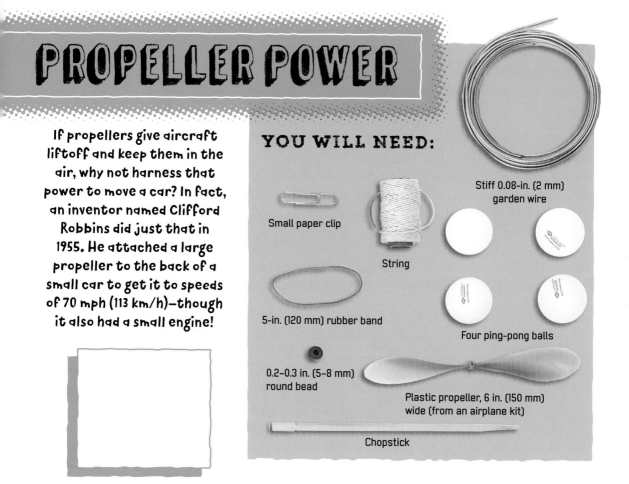

YOU WILL NEED:

Small paper clip

String

5-in. (120 mm) rubber band

0.2–0.3 in. (5–8 mm) round bead

Stiff 0.08-in. (2 mm) garden wire

Four ping-pong balls

Plastic propeller, 6 in. (150 mm) wide (from an airplane kit)

Chopstick

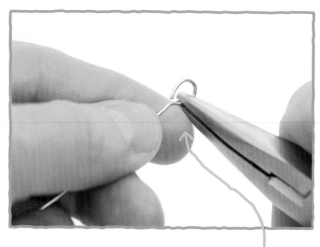

1 Use the pliers to straighten out the paper clip and bend a loop in the end.

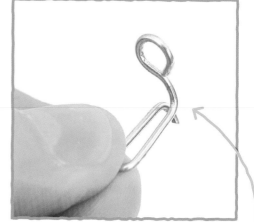

2 Cut a 2.8-in. (70 mm) length of garden wire and make a support in the shape shown.

3 Thread the paper clip wire through the support loop, then through the bead, and finally through the propeller.

4 Bend the end of the paper clip wire to make a right angle to hold it in place. Trim the end with wire cutters.

5 To make the front legs, cut a 14-in. (350 mm) length of garden wire. Use the pliers to bend it symmetrically into the shape shown. The doubled bit is about 0.8 in. (20 mm) long, and roughly at right angles to the legs.

6 Position the legs and propeller support on the end of the chopstick. Wrap string around the end to secure them in place.

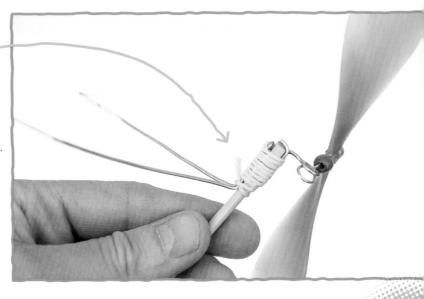

7 Cut another 14-in. (350 mm) piece of wire and shape the back legs as shown. The hook section is about 2 in. (50 mm) long overall. This will stop the legs from being pulled forward.

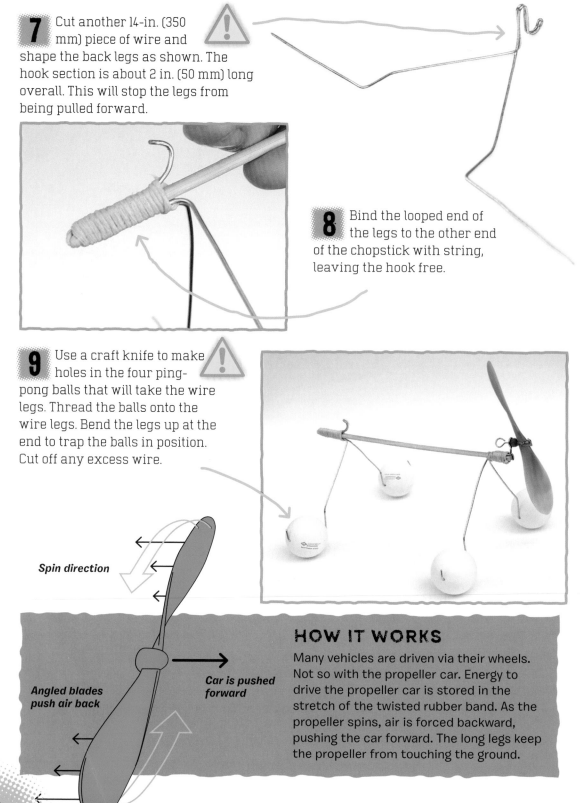

8 Bind the looped end of the legs to the other end of the chopstick with string, leaving the hook free.

9 Use a craft knife to make holes in the four ping-pong balls that will take the wire legs. Thread the balls onto the wire legs. Bend the legs up at the end to trap the balls in position. Cut off any excess wire.

Spin direction

Angled blades push air back

Car is pushed forward

HOW IT WORKS

Many vehicles are driven via their wheels. Not so with the propeller car. Energy to drive the propeller car is stored in the stretch of the twisted rubber band. As the propeller spins, air is forced backward, pushing the car forward. The long legs keep the propeller from touching the ground.

10 Twist the rubber band and fit it between the hook at the back of the car and the loop behind the propeller. Wind up the propeller and . . .

. . . WHOOSH!

REAL-WORLD ENGINEERING

A spinning airplane propeller pushes back masses of air, and this continuous pushing gets the plane moving. A propeller's blades are both twisted and angled. The more steeply they're angled, the more air they push back, and the more the plane moves forward. This also shows Newton's Third Law of Motion in action: a push backward produces a movement forward.

This amazing tricycle has front-wheel drive like lots of cars that have to go over rough terrain. The golf ball wheels work best on a nice smooth surface, though!

TOOLS:
- Scissors
- Utility knife
- File
- Ruler
- Compass
- White glue

YOU WILL NEED:

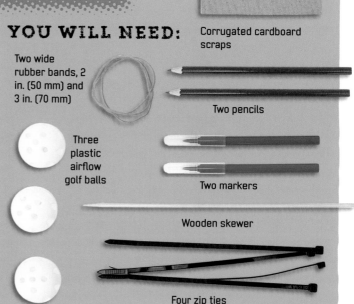

Corrugated cardboard scraps

Two wide rubber bands, 2 in. (50 mm) and 3 in. (70 mm)

Three plastic airflow golf balls

Two pencils

Two markers

Wooden skewer

Four zip ties

1 Cut the 3-in. (70 mm) rubber band and thread it through two symmetrical holes on either side of a ball. Tie the ends together.

2 Use a utility knife to cut a notch near each end of the pencils on one side.

3 Wrap the 2-in. (50 mm) rubber band twice around the ball to create the tire. Thread the pencils through the central rubber band.

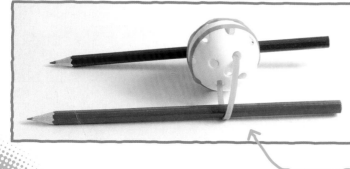

4 Remove the tops and cartridges from the pens. Cut the ends off with a file so they are 4 in. (90 mm) long. Use cable ties to fasten the tubes in the pencil notches.

5 Thread a wooden skewer through the rear tube and slot the two remaining balls in place. Trim the zip ties with scissors.

6 Draw and cut out two cardboard circles, 0.8 in. (20 mm) in diameter, to act as washers. Pierce holes in the centers with the point of the skewer. Glue them in place. Cut off any excess skewer.

Wind up the front wheel by turning it several times— and release!

Z-Z-ZIPP!

HOW IT WORKS

Just like the propeller car, the trike stores its energy in twisted elastic. This time, though, the untwisting drives the front wheel directly, pushing the car forward. The rubber band tire ensures a good grip as the trike moves, just like a car tire on the road surface.

GLOSSARY

ACCELERATION (VERB: ACCELERATE)

The rate at which an object changes speed. Positive acceleration is an increase in speed. Negative acceleration a decrease in speed.

AXLE

A central rod that a vehicle's wheels fit onto and that keeps them an equal distance apart. The axle rotates to make the wheels rotate so the vehicle can move.

CHEMICAL ENERGY

The energy stored in chemical compounds, which is released by a chemical reaction. For example, when wood burns (creating a chemical reaction), the chemical energy turns into heat and light energy. Batteries, natural gas and petroleum, all have masses of stored chemical energy.

ELECTRICAL ENERGY

The energy that moves charged particles through a wire. This flow of energy is called a current and can be converted to perform all sorts of work such as making light, heat, or sound. An electric motor converts electrical energy into kinetic energy, the energy of motion.

ENERGY

The ability to apply force to move an object or do work

FRICTION

A force that works against an object sliding along a surface. For example, a ball rolling along a road will eventually stop because of friction from the road's surface.

GEARS

The circular, interlocking wheels in an engine that help to control the vehicle's speed. They work with the throttle, which controls the speed at which the engine rotates. The range of speed in first gear might go up to 15 mph (24 km/h), in second up to 25 mph (40 km/h), in third up to 40 mph (64 km/h), and so on. A lower gear therefore gives more power, and a higher gear gives more speed.

GRAVITY

The force that pulls objects toward one another. The larger the object, the stronger its force of gravity. This is why things stay in place on Earth's surface unless they are shot off, with a huge amount of force, into space.

KINETIC ENERGY

The energy that all moving objects have. The amount of energy depends on an object's mass and speed.

NEWTON'S THIRD LAW OF MOTION

The physical law that states that every action has an equal and opposite reaction—that is, a push backward creates an equal push forward, or vice versa. The great scientist Isaac Newton published this law in 1687, along with his first two laws about how forces relate to motion.

PROJECTILE

Any object fired or thrown into the air by a force

RESTORING FORCE

The force that returns a system or material to its original shape or position after it has been pulled or misshapen. For example, a spring that has been elongated will return to its natural shape and length by its own restoring force.

THE AUTHOR

Rob Ives is a former math and science teacher, currently a designer and paper engineer living in Cumbria, UK. He creates science- and project-based children's books, including *Paper Models that Rock!* and *Paper Automata*. He specializes in character-based paper animations and all kinds of fun and fascinating science projects, and he often visits schools to talk about design technology and to demonstrate his models. Rob's other series for Hungry Tomato include *Tabletop Battles* and *Amazing Science Experiments*.

Picture Credits
(abbreviations: t = top; b = bottom; c = center;
l = left; r = right)
Shutterstock.com: Alex Mit 15br, Anatoly
Vartanov 29br, bunnyphoto 23br, Dmitry
Minein 6tr, Igor Maltsev 19br, John A Davis 11br
& 31tr, nikkytok 9br & 31tl, Phillip Rubino 17bl,
Radoslaw Maciejewski 27bl.